j912
M83s

W9-DFO-659

3 5674 02286957 3

DETROIT PUBLIC LIBRARY

Knapp Branch Library
13330 Conant
Detroit, MI 48212

DATE DUE

SEP 0 5 1995

JAN 0 4 1997

NOV 1 5 1999

OCT 1 8 2000

NOV 2 8 2000

BC-3

MAR 95

KN

THE STUDENT'S
ACTIVITY ATLAS

NEIL MORRIS

Gareth Stevens Publishing
MILWAUKEE

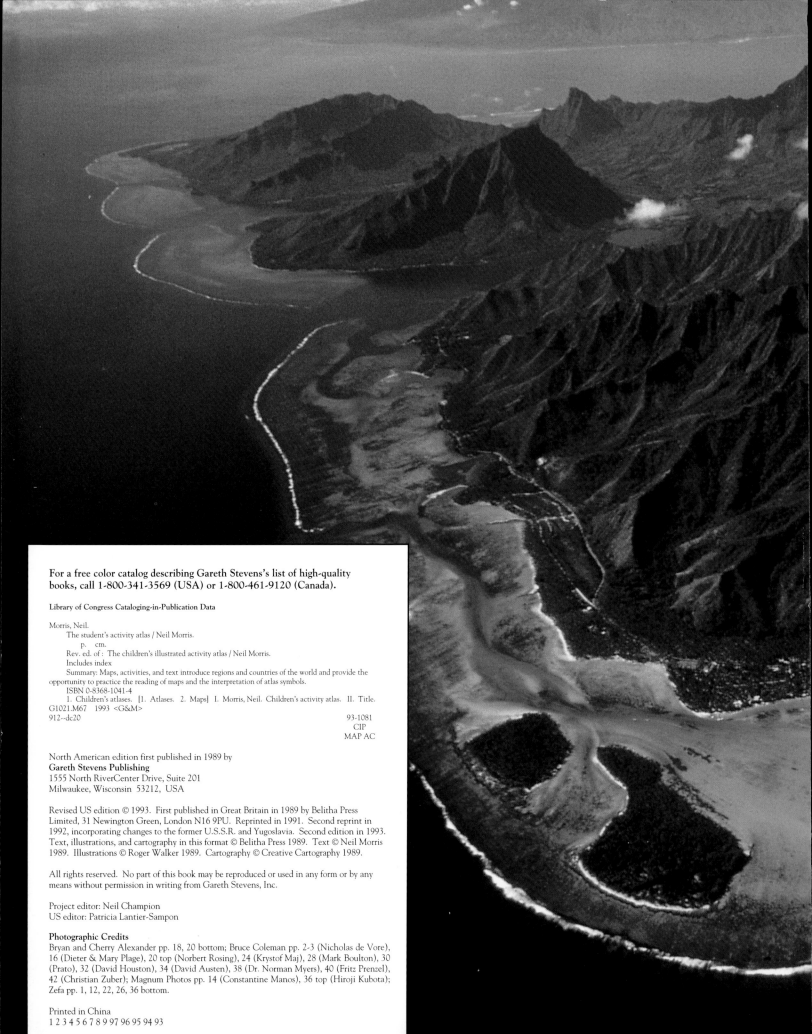

For a free color catalog describing Gareth Stevens's list of high-quality
books, call 1-800-341-3569 (USA) or 1-800-461-9120 (Canada).

Library of Congress Cataloging-in-Publication Data

Morris, Neil.
     The student's activity atlas / Neil Morris.
        p.   cm.
     Rev. ed. of : The children's illustrated activity atlas / Neil Morris.
     Includes index
     Summary: Maps, activities, and text introduce regions and countries of the world and provide the
opportunity to practice the reading of maps and the interpretation of atlas symbols.
     ISBN 0-8368-1041-4
     1. Children's atlases. [1. Atlases. 2. Maps] I. Morris, Neil. Children's activity atlas. II. Title.
G1021.M67 1993 <G&M>
912--dc20   93-1081
                                                                                   CIP
                                                                                 MAP AC

North American edition first published in 1989 by
Gareth Stevens Publishing
1555 North RiverCenter Drive, Suite 201
Milwaukee, Wisconsin 53212, USA

Revised US edition © 1993. First published in Great Britain in 1989 by Belitha Press
Limited, 31 Newington Green, London N16 9PU. Reprinted in 1991. Second reprint in
1992, incorporating changes to the former U.S.S.R. and Yugoslavia. Second edition in 1993.
Text, illustrations, and cartography in this format © Belitha Press 1989. Text © Neil Morris
1989. Illustrations © Roger Walker 1989. Cartography © Creative Cartography 1989.

All rights reserved. No part of this book may be reproduced or used in any form or by any
means without permission in writing from Gareth Stevens, Inc.

Project editor: Neil Champion
US editor: Patricia Lantier-Sampon

Photographic Credits
Bryan and Cherry Alexander pp. 18, 20 bottom; Bruce Coleman pp. 2-3 (Nicholas de Vore),
16 (Dieter & Mary Plage), 20 top (Norbert Rosing), 24 (Krystof Maj), 28 (Mark Boulton), 30
(Prato), 32 (David Houston), 34 (David Austen), 38 (Dr. Norman Myers), 40 (Fritz Prenzel),
42 (Christian Zuber); Magnum Photos pp. 14 (Constantine Manos), 36 top (Hiroji Kubota);
Zefa pp. 1, 12, 22, 26, 36 bottom.

Printed in China
1 2 3 4 5 6 7 8 9 97 96 95 94 93

Contents

What is a map?

A map is an accurately drawn picture of the things around us on Earth's surface. Maps are very useful because they show the shape of the land, the distances between different places, and the best way to get from one place to another.

Some maps show only a very small part of Earth. These maps may indicate your school or the town where you live. Other maps show entire regions, countries, or continents.

1

2

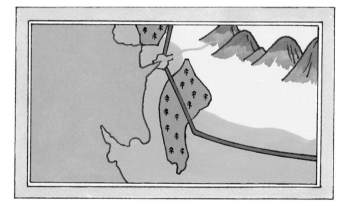

3

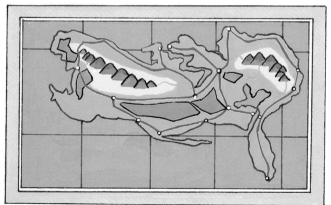

Map 1 is a close-up of map 2, showing the area around the bridge in detail. Map 3 uses a much smaller scale. In the same area on the page, it can show the entire island (you can just see the bridge on the western end of the island).

The globe shows the shape of Earth as it really is. But a map changes this round shape into a flat shape so the entire Earth can be seen at once.

Maps put dry land, wet sea, high mountains, and low plains on sheets of flat paper. It is not very easy to do this. A whole town, country, or even the world needs to fit onto the sheet of paper. This is done by using what is known as *scale* (see page 8).

In reality, the world is shaped like a ball. It is impossible to see the entire ball from one view. To see it all, it first has to be flattened out (see page 5).

Also, because things on Earth's surface have been made smaller (using scale), they cannot be shown as they really look. So people who make maps use symbols (see page 9). Symbols are simple shapes and colors that stand for something in the real world: a capital city, a range of mountains, a sheep farm, or your school.

Making Earth flat

The whole surface of a ball cannot be shown on a flat sheet of paper without cutting and stretching the ball. This is what we have to do to show the surface of Earth as a map.

If we pretend that Earth is an orange, we can divide it into segments. Even though the segments are not flat, we can see the entire orange at once if we lay the segments out. Before we cut the orange, we can put a sticky label around it, as shown below. This will help us understand how a round shape becomes distorted when it is flattened out.

Look what has happened to the sticky label. To get rid of the cuts or gaps and to bring the cut parts back together, we have to stretch the pieces so they touch one another, like this:

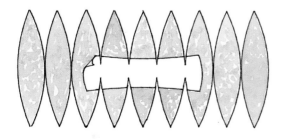

We could lay the segments in another pattern, like this:

Or we could arrange to have a special sticky label made in this shape:

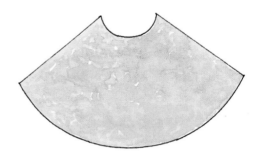

Whatever way we arrange the segments, we cannot show them as they are on the surface of a round object. We have to distort them to make them flat. This means that in making maps, we have to accept the fact that distances and direction change slightly.

These pictures show how the shape of Australia can change by stretching it flat in different ways. Compare these maps with the map of Australia on page 41. Different ways of stretching are called *projections*.

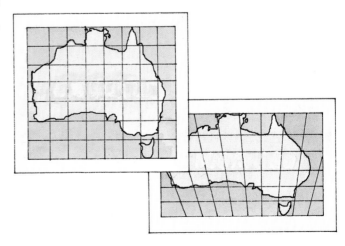

Finding the direction

Maps have a language you can learn. Map language begins with four basic directions: north, south, east, and west. These directions answer the question, "Which way?"

North is the direction toward the North Pole from any place on Earth. South is toward the South Pole in the opposite direction. As we face north, the direction to the right is called east. This is where the Sun appears every morning. The direction to the left as we face north is called west.

North is usually at the top of a map. If we want to find out which direction north is, we use a compass. The needle of a compass always points north. Once we know which direction north is, we can easily figure out the other directions.

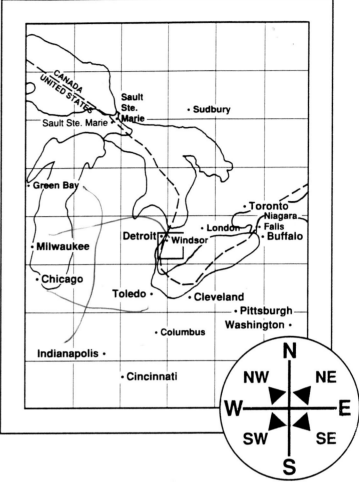

Using a compass, can you find out in which direction you have to travel from Detroit or Windsor to get to the other places marked on the map?

This map shows how the points of a compass can be used to divide the continent of Africa.

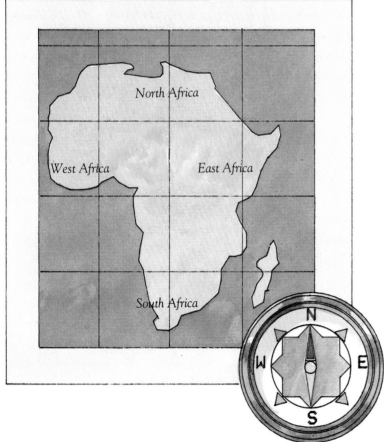

We can describe other directions, too. Halfway between north and east is a direction called northeast. Halfway between east and south is called southeast.

Direction and distance can be used to describe the position of a place. For example, you could describe a city as being 100 miles (160 kilometers) east of where you are. We can also divide areas, countries, and continents according to their compass position. For example, we talk of South Africa, which is a country in Africa, or eastern Africa, central Africa, and northern Africa, which are regions of the African continent made up of many small countries.

Knowing where we are

Every place in the world has a particular position where it can always be found. You can find buildings and people by using their addresses. You have an address where your mail is delivered. But what is the "address" of a city, a mountain, a forest, or an entire country?

Look at the picture below. It shows a city, a mountain, and a forest. It also has a grid of lines on it with numbers and letters down the side and along the top. Using these lines, we can give each place an address of sorts: the city is at A2, the mountain peak at B1, and the forest at C3. To find the address, follow the lines to their numbers and letters and put them together.

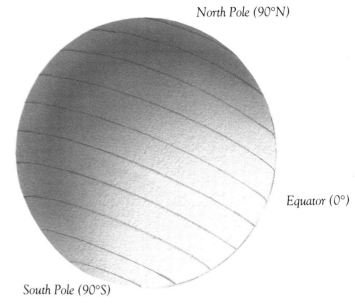

North Pole (90°N)

Equator (0°)

South Pole (90°S)

The lines of latitude

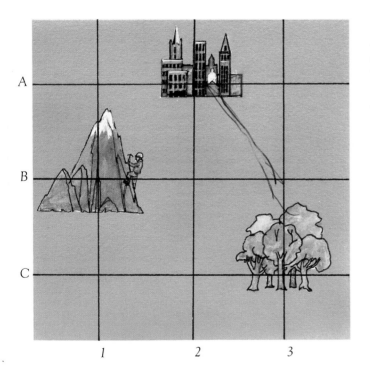

Maps use imaginary lines called latitude and longitude to divide the world. Lines of latitude are circles drawn around the globe. They measure how far north or south a place is. All the lines of latitude run parallel to the Equator. They are given a number (a degree or °) north or south of the Equator. They reach a maximum of 90° north at the North Pole and 90° south at the South Pole.

Lines of longitude are imaginary lines running up and down the globe from the North Pole to the South Pole. They measure in degrees how far east or west a place is from a line known as the Greenwich Meridian in London, England. This point is longitude zero. Lines of longitude are measured up to 180° east and 180° west.

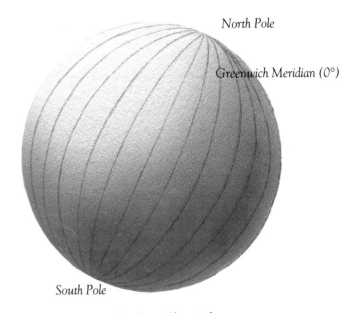

North Pole

Greenwich Meridian (0°)

South Pole

The lines of longitude

7

Using the scale bar

The scale of a toy car is the difference in size between it and the real thing. This toy car is 4 inches (10 cm) long, and the real car on which it is based is 160 inches (400 cm) long. This means that 1 inch on the toy equals 16 inches on the real car. We say the toy has a scale of 1:16. The real car is 16 times bigger than the toy.

A map scale is used in the same way. A scale of 1:1,000 means that a distance of 1 inch on the map is actually 1,000 inches on real ground. This works the same with metrics. So *scale* is the system that brings things down to sizes that fit on paper. Scale lets you hold thousands of square miles or kilometers on a map in your hand.

To make things easier to understand, maps usually have a scale bar, where the measured distance and the real ground distance are matched to each other.

On each map in this atlas, there is a scale bar shown as a ruler. One side of the ruler shows centimeters and kilometers, and the other side shows inches and miles. The scale varies from map to map, so be careful when using it!

You can measure distances on your maps by using paper. Put the edge of the paper along a line running between two points on the map. Put a mark by each point. Then put the paper on the scale bar and read off the real distance between the two points.

0	500	1000	1500	2000	2500 KILOMETERS

CENTIMETERS
INCHES

Using the symbols

All maps use symbols. Symbols are simple images that stand for something else more complicated in the real world. For example, if we want to show an area where cotton grows, we can show it using a symbol like the one in the picture on the right. We can imagine what a real cotton field looks like when we see the symbol on the map. But first we need to know what the symbols stand for. We can guess the meaning of some. Others may be more difficult.

Different maps use different symbols. The maps in this atlas use only a few symbols to show you some of the interesting things that go on in the world. But the world is a very complicated place, and there are many other products and activities in these countries that are not shown using our symbols.

Here are the symbols used in this atlas and the meanings of the differently colored landscapes:

Cotton symbol

Cotton picking

- ⚓ Major port
- ✈ International airport
- ➤ Fishing zone
- 🌾 Grain farming
- 🍇 Vineyards (Grapes)
- ⚘ Cotton fields
- 🎋 Sugar plantations
- ✦ Cattle farming
- 🐕 Sheep farming
- ⚲ Goat herding
- ⚑ Rubber plantations

- ⛏ Coal mining
- 🛢 Oil wells
- 🔥 Gas
- ≈ Dam
- ⚙ Heavy industry
- 🐘 Game reserve
- ■ Capital city
- ◻ Important town or city
- △ Mountain peak

Mountains

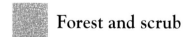
Forest and scrub

Desert

Farmland

Frozen landscape
(snow and ice)

9

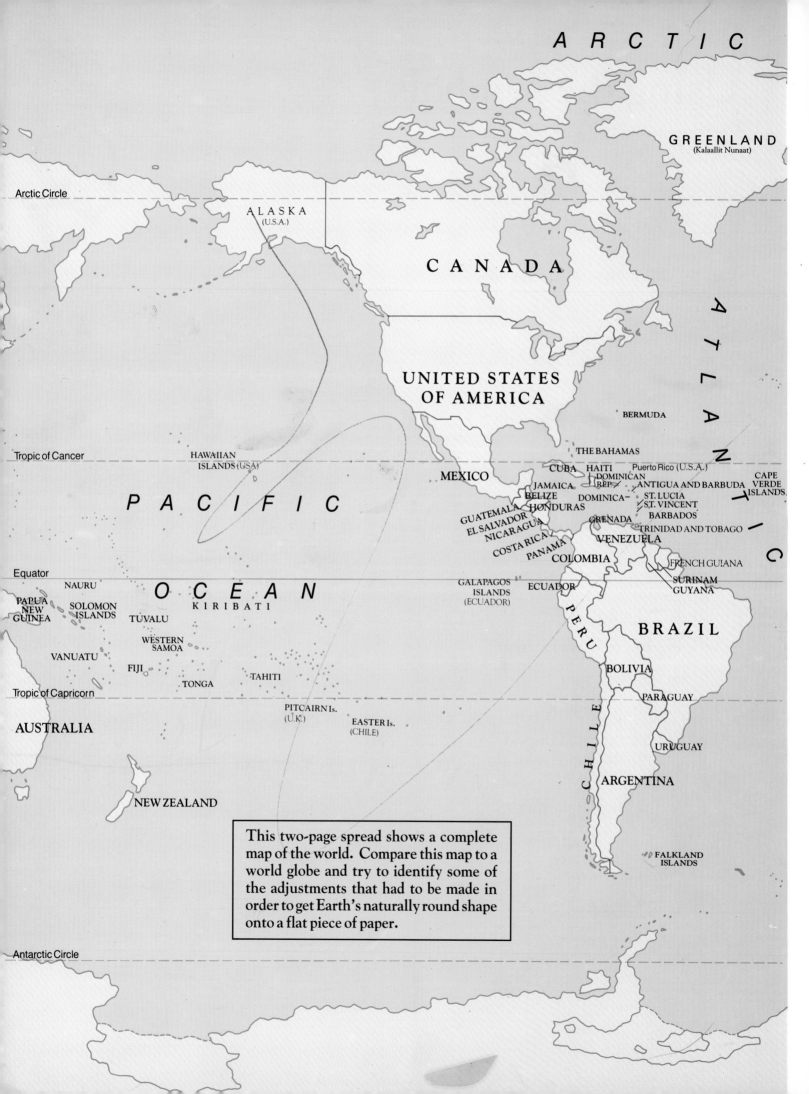

ARCTIC

GREENLAND
(Kalaallit Nunaat)

Arctic Circle

ALASKA
(U.S.A.)

CANADA

A
T
L
A
N
T
I
C

UNITED STATES
OF AMERICA

BERMUDA

Tropic of Cancer

HAWAIIAN
ISLANDS (USA)

THE BAHAMAS

MEXICO

CUBA   HAITI   Puerto Rico (U.S.A.)
              DOMINICAN
JAMAICA   REP.   ANTIGUA AND BARBUDA   CAPE
       BELIZE   DOMINICA–   VERDE
GUATEMALA   HONDURAS   ST. LUCIA   ISLANDS
EL SALVADOR   ST. VINCENT
      NICARAGUA   GRENADA BARBADOS
COSTA RICA   TRINIDAD AND TOBAGO
        PANAMA   VENEZUELA

P A C I F I C

Equator

GALAPAGOS
ISLANDS
(ECUADOR)

ECUADOR

COLOMBIA

FRENCH GUIANA
SURINAM
GUYANA

NAURU

O C E A N

K I R I B A T I

PAPUA
NEW
GUINEA

SOLOMON
ISLANDS

TUVALU

PERU

BRAZIL

VANUATU

WESTERN
SAMOA

FIJI

TONGA

TAHITI

BOLIVIA

Tropic of Capricorn

PITCAIRN Is.
(U.K.)

EASTER Is.
(CHILE)

PARAGUAY

AUSTRALIA

C
H
I
L
E

URUGUAY

ARGENTINA

NEW ZEALAND

FALKLAND
ISLANDS

This two-page spread shows a complete
map of the world. Compare this map to a
world globe and try to identify some of
the adjustments that had to be made in
order to get Earth's naturally round shape
onto a flat piece of paper.

Antarctic Circle

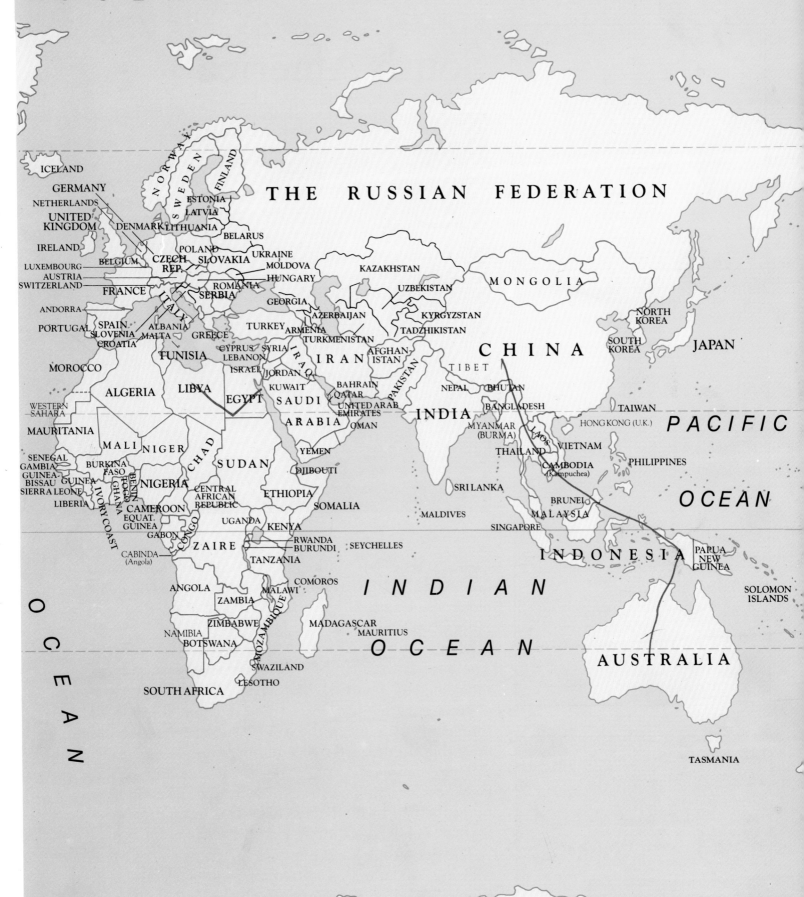

Right: Peru's Lake Titicaca is the world's highest lake. People living around the lake make boats from the reeds that grow there.

South America

Activities

- How far is it from Brasília to Buenos Aires?

- Which is the largest country in South America?

- The Equator runs through three South American countries. Which are they?

- Which six countries lie on longitude 60°W? And which islands?

- In which ocean is the mouth of the Amazon River?

- What is the capital of Venezuela?

- Mount Chimborazo is an extinct volcano in the Andes. How high is it?

- How many countries are there in South America?

Regional Facts

Population: 283 million people

Largest Country: Brazil

Smallest Country: French Guiana

Largest City: Buenos Aires, Argentina 10 million people

Highest Mountain: Aconcagua, Argentina, 22,831 feet (6,959 m)

Longest River: Amazon, 4,000 miles (6,440 km) — the second longest river in the world

South America is a continent of very different landscapes. The Andes mountain range runs near the Pacific coast along the length of the continent. It is nearly 5,500 miles (9,000 km) long.

More than half of South America is covered by forest. The huge Amazonian rain forest stretches over parts of nine different countries. More than 2,500 different types of trees grow in this forest. The Amazon River flows through it. It is one of the world's largest rivers and has more than 1,000 small rivers running into it.

The Atacama Desert is one of the driest places on Earth. Some parts have never had any rain. The southern tip of the continent is very cold. It is not far from the harsh, frozen land of Antarctica.

The first people to live in South America were tribal Indians. About 400 years ago, Spanish and Portuguese people landed on the continent and colonized different areas. Today, most of the people in South America speak Spanish or Portuguese, although Indian languages are still spoken in some areas.

Central America, Mexico, and the Caribbean

Children in Mexico display a tempting selection of foods.

Regional Facts

Population: 136 million people

Largest Country: Mexico

Largest City: Mexico City, Mexico, 18 million people

Highest Mountain: Citlaltepetl, Mexico, 18,697 feet (5,699 m)

Longest River: Rio Grande, 1,267 miles (2,040 km)

Actually part of North America, Mexico is the largest country in this region. It is almost four times bigger than the other countries of the area put together. At the southern end of Central America, the Panama Canal joins the Caribbean Sea to the Pacific Ocean.

Two-thirds of the people of this area are *mestizos*. They are a mixture of the Indians who originally lived here and the Europeans who came to find gold. Europeans brought Christianity with them, but in some areas traditional Indian religions are still practiced.

In the Caribbean Sea, a group of islands stretches in a crescent shape from Florida in the U.S. to Venezuela in South America. Cuba is the largest island, and nearly half of the Caribbean island people live in either Cuba or Haiti.

The people of the Caribbean come from many ethnic backgrounds. Many are descended from slaves brought from Africa to work on sugar plantations. The islands have a warm, tropical climate that attracts tourists. Most people work on farms or in hotels, shops, and small factories. Farmers grow fruit, sugar cane, cotton, and coffee.

Activities

- What is the capital of Honduras?
- How far is it from Tijuana to Monterrey?
- How many countries are there in Central America?
- In which direction do you travel from Monterrey to Mexico City?
- Which is the largest island in the Caribbean Sea?
- Which ocean is to the north of the West Indies?
- Which four countries border on Guatemala?
- Which republic shares an island with Haiti?
- How high is the highest mountain in Guatemala?
- Which Central American country lies on latitude 10°N?

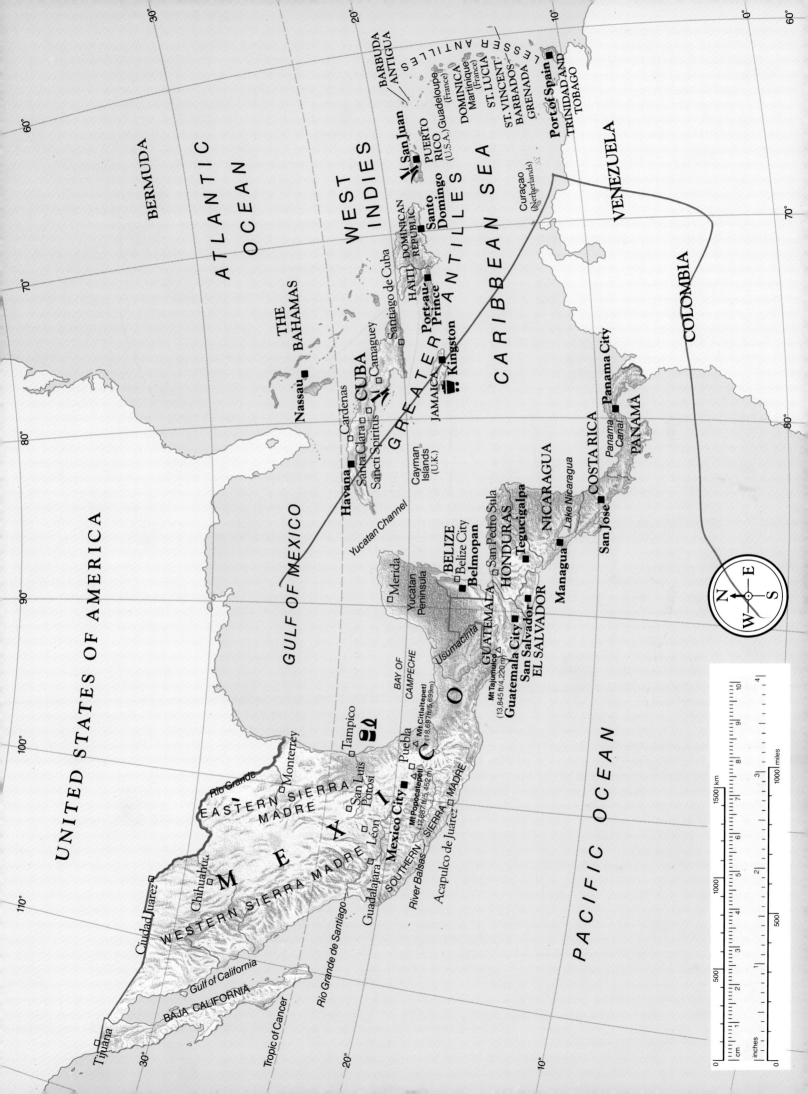

United States of America (lower forty-eight states)

The United States of America (U.S.A.) is one of the largest and richest countries in the world. It is made up of fifty states, each with its own capital city. The U.S. flag has fifty stars (one for each of the states) and thirteen stripes (for the original thirteen colonies). Alaska joined in January 1959 to become the largest state, followed by Hawaii in August 1959.

People were already living in this land before any European settlers came. They were the American Indians. The first European immigrants settled in what is now the United States almost 400 years ago. They came from England and called the wild new land New England. Others came from Spain and Holland, naming the places they colonized after familiar cities and towns they had left behind. There were many battles between Europeans and Indians, until the Europeans controlled almost all the land.

Today, the U.S. has a mix of peoples, including the American Indians, African-Americans, Europeans (such as Spanish, British, Dutch, German, French, Irish, Italian, and Polish), Latin Americans, Asians, and more. This mixture of cultures gives the country a rich variety of lifestyles, food, music, and art.

Regional Facts

Population: 240 million people

Capital: Washington, D.C., 3.5 million people

Largest City: New York, 7 million people

Highest Mountain: Mt. McKinley, Alaska, 20,318 feet (6,193 m) (see page 19)

Longest River: Missouri, 2,713 miles (4,367 km)

The United States is the fourth largest country in the world.

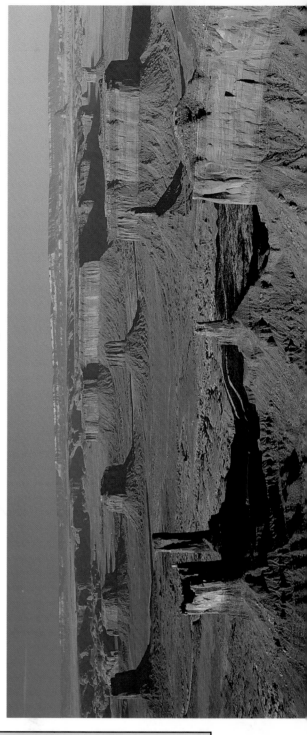

The United States has spectacular natural scenery as well as great cities. This is Monument Valley in Arizona.

Activities

- How far is it by direct flight from New Orleans to Miami?

- The smallest state lies between Massachusetts and Connecticut. What is it?

- Which ocean is to the west of the mainland United States?

- Which state is just to the east of Arizona?

- What is the highest mountain in the lower forty-eight states, and what famous city is it close to?

- What is the capital of the U.S.?

- In which state is the Grand Canyon?

- On what river is the Hoover Dam?

- What are the main mountain ranges in the lower forty-eight states?

- Which state is split in two by a lake?

Canada, Alaska (U.S.), and Greenland

Polar bears roam the cold Canadian north.

Much of Canada is very cold and snow-covered in winter. In the north, in the Arctic Ocean, is a group of large, ice-covered islands, where very few people live. To the south of the islands are vast areas of pine forest. Most Canadians live in the country's southernmost part, near the Great Lakes and the St. Lawrence River.

To the northwest of the Great Lakes are Canada's prairies, where enormous wheat farms stretch as far as the eye can see. Farther west are the high Rocky Mountains, which stretch down into the United States.

American Indians and the Inuit (Eskimos) were Canada's original inhabitants. Now, most Canadians are of British and French descent.

Canada is one of the world's richest countries. Wheat farming, wood, fish, oil, gas, and minerals bring wealth to this modern nation.

Alaska is joined to Canada but is a part of the United States. It is the largest of the fifty states in area, but very few people live there because it is mostly frozen and barren.

Greenland is nearly covered by a huge ice cap, making it the world's largest ice mass outside of Antarctica. Because of its extreme climate and geography, only about 54,000 people live in Greenland.

Regional Facts

Population: 25 million people

Capital (Canada): Ottawa, 285,000 people

Largest City (Canada): Montréal, 980,000 people

Highest Mountain (in Canada): Mt. Logan, 19,850 ft (6,050 m)

Longest River: Mackenzie, 1,120 miles (1,800 km)

Largest Lake: Superior, the largest freshwater lake in the world

Canada is the second largest country in the world.

Greenland is the largest island in the world.

Activities

- In which province is Calgary?
- On which lake is Yellowknife?
- Which two islands lie on the Arctic Circle?
- How far is it from Winnipeg to Montréal?
- Which ocean lies to the west of Canada?
- Can you find London in Canada?
- Between which two lakes are the Niagara Falls?
- In which direction do you travel from Sudbury to Montréal?
- In which bay do latitude 60°N and longitude 85°W meet?

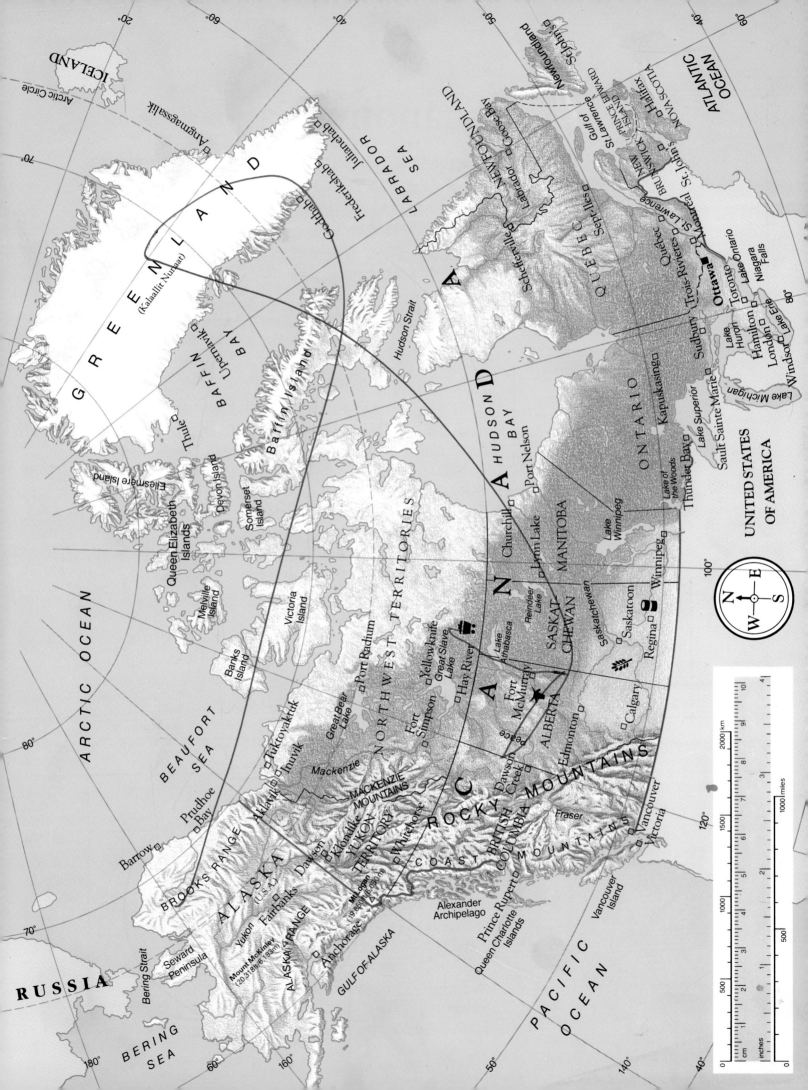

Scandinavia

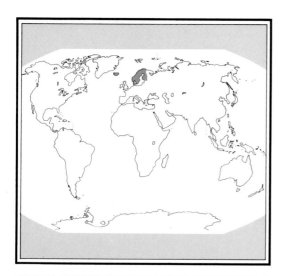

A village in the Lofoten Islands of northern Norway. Fishing is an important part of the economy.

Activities

- Which Scandinavian country is farthest from the Arctic Circle?
- What is the capital of Iceland?
- In which direction do you travel from Malmö to Stockholm?
- Which Swedish town is directly east of Copenhagen?
- Which gulf separates Sweden and Finland?
- How far is it from Oslo to Copenhagen?
- In which ocean is Iceland?
- Approximately how far is it across Iceland from east to west?
- Which latitude touches the northern tip of Iceland?
- Which Scandinavian country has the northernmost point?

Denmark, Sweden, Norway, Iceland, and Finland make up the part of Europe called Scandinavia. Denmark is made up of a peninsula, called Jutland, and about 100 small islands. Denmark is known around the world for its rich farmland.

Sweden and Finland are covered with thick forests. The paper industry in Sweden is very important. Huge mills turn wood from the forests into paper. Finland is peppered with lakes. There are about 60,000 in all. Norway is very mountainous. Large glaciers in the last Ice Age cut deep, narrow inlets of the sea, called fiords, into the coastline. Many fishing trawlers leave the coastal towns to gather their catch of fish in the North Sea.

Northern Scandinavia is sometimes called "the land of the midnight Sun." Because this land is so far north, beyond the Arctic Circle, the Sun shines all through the night for a few days each summer. In winter, the opposite is true: for a few days each season, the Sun does not rise above the horizon.

Iceland is an island that lies just south of the Arctic Circle. As in Norway, fishing is a very important industry to the people who live there. The landscape is frozen and covered in parts by glaciers. Yet Iceland is home to active volcanoes and hot springs that bubble up from under Earth's surface.

Regional Facts

Population: 25 million people

Largest Country: Sweden

Smallest Country: Denmark

Largest City: Stockholm, Sweden, 1.5 million people

Highest Mountain: Galdhoppigen, Norway, 8, 103 feet (2,469 m)

Longest River: Glama, Norway, 380 miles (611 km)

A Lapp woman with a herd of reindeer.

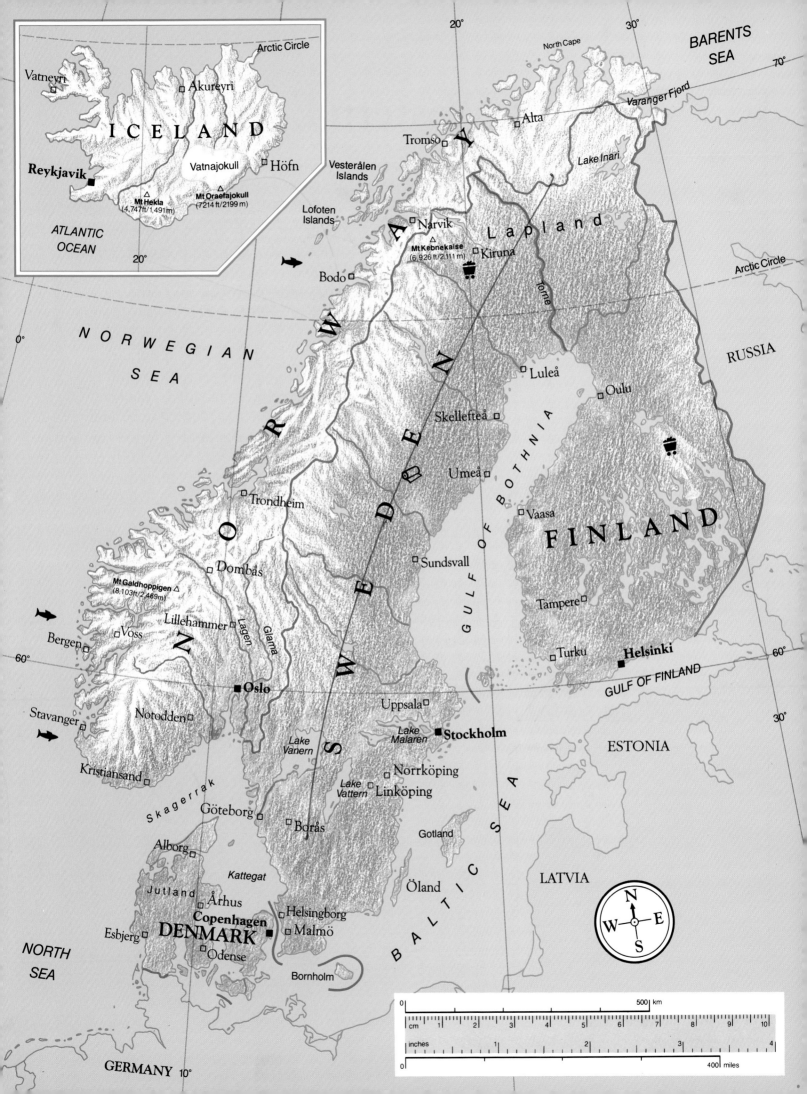

ICELAND

Vatneyri

Akureyri

Arctic Circle

Vatnajokull

Reykjavik · Höfn

Mt Hekla
(4,747ft/1,491m)

Mt Oraefajokull
(7214 ft/2199 m)

ATLANTIC
OCEAN

20°

20°

30°

BARENTS
SEA

70°

North Cape

Varanger Fjord

Alta

Tromso

Lake Inari

N O R W A Y

Lapland

Vesterålen
Islands

Narvik

Lofoten
Islands

Mt Kebnekaise
(6,926 ft/2,111 m)

Kiruna

Torne

Arctic Circle

Bodo

RUSSIA

N O R W E G I A N

S E A

Luleå

Oulu

S W E D E N

Skellefteå

GULF OF BOTHNIA

0°

Trondheim

Umeå

FINLAND

Mt Galdhoppigen
(8,103ft/2,469m)

Dombås

Vaasa

Sundsvall

Lillehammer

Lagen

Glama

Bergen

Voss

N O R W A Y

Turku

Helsinki

Tampere

60°

60°

Oslo

GULF OF FINLAND

Stavanger

Notodden

Uppsala

30°

Lake
Vanern

Lake
Malaren

Stockholm

ESTONIA

Kristiansand

Norrköping

Lake
Vattern

Linköping

Skagerrak

Göteborg

Borås

Gotland

B A L T I C   S E A

LATVIA

Alborg

Kattegat

Öland

Jutland

Århus

Helsingborg

Copenhagen

DENMARK

Malmö

Esbjerg

Odense

NORTH
SEA

Bornholm

GERMANY

10°

N
W E
S

0										500	km

cm 1 2 3 4 5 6 7 8 9 10

inches 1 2 3 4

0   400 miles

Western Europe

Industry is very important to the countries of western Europe, and the area's factory goods are sold throughout the world. Farming is also very important. Grapes and olives are two of the many products grown in the warm Mediterranean countries (Italy, France, Portugal, and Spain). Dairy produce and grain are more common in the colder, wetter countries like Germany and Britain.

France is the largest country in Europe. It has always been popular with vacationers for its varied landscape, warm climate, good food and wine, and beautiful cities. Switzerland and Austria are mountainous. Winter skiing in the Alps attracts many people from other countries. The Low Countries are Belgium, the Netherlands, and Luxembourg. Some land in the Netherlands is below sea level. Banks of earth, called dikes, have been built to keep the sea from flooding the fertile land behind them.

Spain and Portugal are also popular countries for tourists. Portugal is the world's leading producer of cork, which comes from the bark of a tree grown in that country. Spain was ruled by the Romans for over 600 years, and the remains of their buildings and walls can still be seen throughout the country. The Arabs also conquered parts of Spain in the Middle Ages. One of their most famous sites is the Alhambra in Granada, in southern Spain.

Activities

- Which islands lie to the east of Valencia, Spain?
- What is the longitude of London?
- Which three countries border on Luxembourg?
- Which river flows through Paris?
- What is the capital of Portugal?
- In which direction do you travel from Paris to Barcelona?
- Which four countries make up the United Kingdom?
- Which mountain range separates France from Spain?
- How far is it from London to Edinburgh?
- Which sea is to the east of Scotland?

Regional Facts

Population: 300 million people

Largest Country: France

Largest City: Paris, France, 10 million people

Highest Mountain: Mont Blanc, France, 15,771 feet (4,807 m)

Longest River: Rhine, 820 miles (1,320 km)

Right: Rotterdam is one of many large ports along the coast of western Europe.

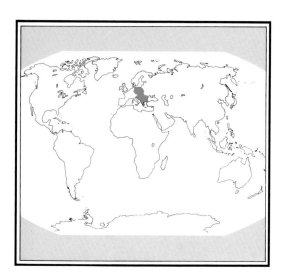

Eastern Europe

The peoples in this part of Europe have many different customs and histories. Ancient Greek writers and philosophers influenced all of Europe with their ideas. In eastern Europe, many ancient Greek buildings still remain, such as the Parthenon in Athens.

Yugoslavia's breakup into smaller countries has been accompanied by fierce fighting as new countries struggle for territory. The people of Czechoslovakia also decided to split their country. The former Czechoslovakia is now two separate countries: Czech Republic and Slovakia.

Poland is the largest country in this part of Europe, with ports on the Baltic Sea. It has many large industries and produces a lot of coal. The Czech Republic, Slovakia, and Hungary do not have a coastline. They use the Danube River to transport goods. The Danube River also forms part of the boundary between Romania and Bulgaria before it finally flows into the Black Sea.

The countryside is a mixture of flat plains for raising crops and animals and mountain ranges with sheltered valleys and winding rivers.

Activities

- Which Greek island is farthest south?
- What is the capital of Poland?
- Which river flows through Budapest, the capital of Hungary?
- In which country is Lake Balaton?
- Over which countries do the Carpathian Mountains stretch?
- In which direction do you travel to get from Belgrade to Bucharest?
- Which five countries lie on longitude 20° E?
- Into which sea does the Danube River flow?

Right: Most of the city of Warsaw in Poland was destroyed during World War II and had to be rebuilt.

Regional Facts

Population: 200 million people

Largest Country: Poland

Smallest Country: Albania

Largest City: Athens, Greece, 3 million people

Highest Mountain: Mt. Olympus, Greece, 9,570 feet (2,918 m)

Longest River: Danube, 1,770 miles (2,850 km)

Northern Africa

The vast Sahara Desert stretches across almost the whole of northern Africa, covering part or all of thirteen countries. It is the largest desert in the world. Scattered across the desert are oases, where water is found. Many are single small springs with a few palm trees. Nomads who live in the desert bring their animals to drink there.

In the northern part of the Sahara, most people speak Arabic. In Egypt, people live along the fertile Nile valley. The Nile is the longest river in the world, flowing all the way from central Africa to the Mediterranean Sea. The Nile floods once a year. This makes the fields on either side of the river more fertile by leaving behind rich soil. This has helped farmers since ancient times.

The Blue Nile crosses Ethiopia, one of the poorest countries in the world. Somalia, a neighboring country of Ethiopia, is also extremely poor. The people of both countries have suffered widespread famine despite large amounts of foreign aid. Across the African continent, in Nigeria, the situation is very different. The discovery of oil has brought wealth to that country.

Most African nations were once European colonies, but today they are independent nations. Their economic situation depends a lot on natural resources and climate.

Regional Facts

Population: 320 million people

Largest Country: The Sudan

Smallest Country: São Tomé and Principe

Largest City: Cairo, Egypt, 15 million people

Highest Mountain: Ras Dashan, Ethiopia, 15,157 feet (4,620 m)

Longest River: Nile, 4,188 miles (6,741 km) —the longest river in the world

Boats like these feluccas have sailed the Nile River for hundreds of years.

Activities

- How far is it across the Sahara Desert from Algiers to Lagos?

- In which direction do you travel to get from Algiers to Lagos?

- Which four countries border on Lake Chad?

- Is the White Nile west or east of the Blue Nile?

- What is the longitude of Lake Volta, Ghana?

- What is the capital of Ethiopia?

- What is the highest point in the Atlas Mountains, Morocco?

- What seas are connected by the Suez Canal?

- What is the quickest route by sea from Mogadiscio, Somalia, to Italy?

- Name the countries along the coast between Guinea and Nigeria.

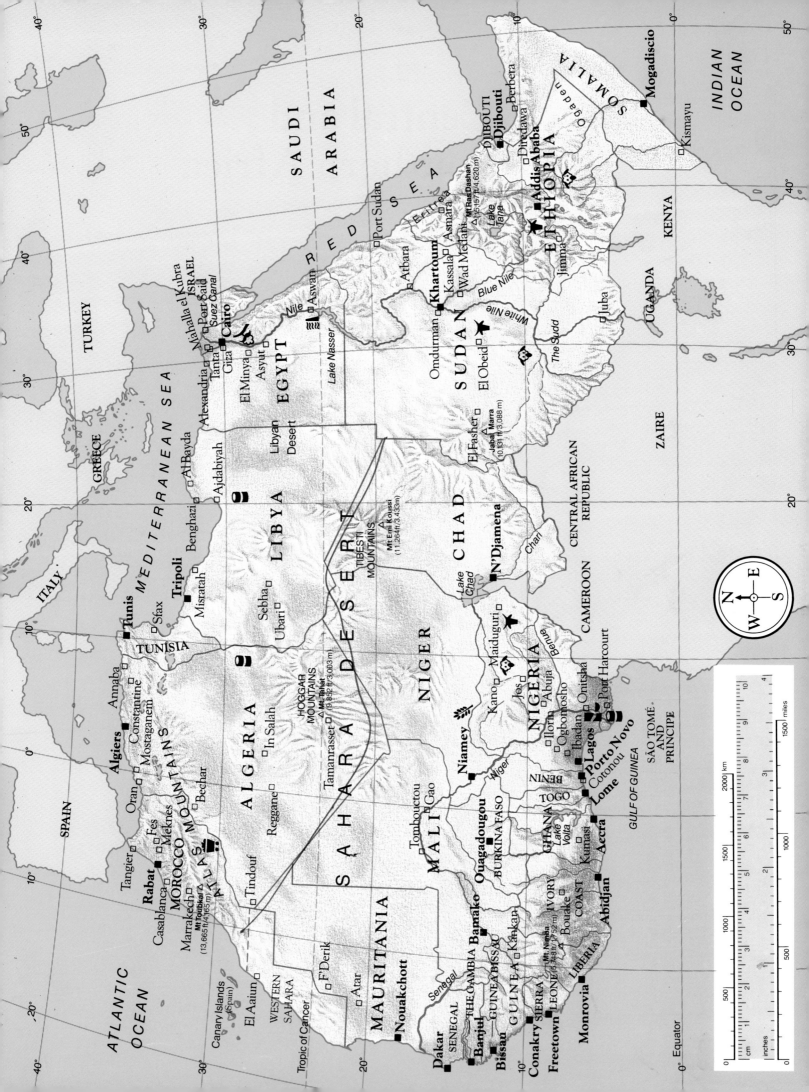

Central and Southern Africa

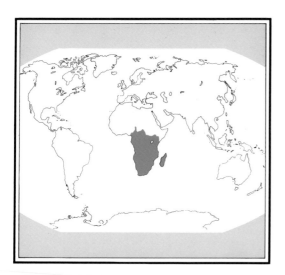

Activities

- Which African country is farthest south?
- Approximately how long is Lake Malawi?
- Which two countries share the Victoria Falls?
- In which direction do you travel to get from Malawi to the Congo?
- How far is it between the peaks of Mount Kenya and Mount Kilimanjaro?
- What is the capital of Burundi?
- Which cape would you sail around to get from Madagascar to Namibia?
- Which lake is formed by the Kariba Dam?
- In which countries is the Kalahari Desert?
- Which six African countries lie on the Equator?

Regional Facts

Population: 200 million people

Largest Country: Zaire (The Congo)

Smallest Country: Comoros

Largest City: Kinshasa, Zaire, 3 million people

Highest Mountain: Kilimanjaro, Tanzania, 19,340 feet (5,895 m)

Longest River: Zaire, 3,000 mi (4,820 km)

Largest Lake: Victoria — the second largest freshwater lake in the world

The city of Nairobi in Kenya.

Much of central Africa is covered by savanna, which is flat grassland with patches of trees and scrub. This is the home of the last great herds of wild animals — lions, giraffes, zebras, elephants, and many others. The nations of eastern Africa, such as Kenya and Tanzania, are famous for their wildlife. People can go on a camera safari and see animals roaming in the wild.

At the heart of southern Africa is the Kalahari desert, where native tribes still live in their traditional way. Often, women collect roots and berries to eat, and men hunt animals with bows and poisoned arrows.

There are many different black African peoples, from the tiny pygmies of the rain forests to the tall Masai of the savanna. Five million whites of European descent live in the Republic of South Africa. Although 80 percent of the people of South Africa are black Africans, they do not yet have an equal right to vote or to elect the national government.

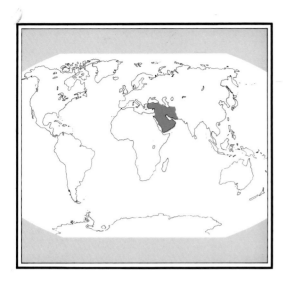

Southwest Asia

This region, which is part of the Middle East, is sometimes called "the cradle of civilization." Some of the most ancient civilizations were born here, as well as three major religions — Christianity, Islam, and Judaism. Three continents also meet here — Europe, Asia, and Africa.

Most people in this region are Arabs. They are Muslims, followers of Islam, and their language is Arabic. Turkey and Iran are non-Arabic nations, but most of the people there are Muslims. Their god is Allah, and his prophet is Muhammed.

There are Christians in Cyprus and Lebanon, and most people in Israel are Jewish. The ancient Holy Land of Palestine (where Israel and Jordan are today) is sacred to Jews, Muslims, and Christians.

Much of Southwest Asia is desert. It is very hot during the day and cold at night. The discovery of oil has made countries like Saudi Arabia, Bahrain, Qatar, Kuwait, and Iran very wealthy. Large ships, called oil tankers, take oil from the Persian Gulf to Europe through the Red Sea and the Suez Canal.

A colorful mosque in Iran. Priests call the people to prayer from the towers.

Activities

- Which country forms the north-eastern coast of the Persian Gulf?
- In which direction do you sail from Aden, Yemen, to the island of Socotra?
- Which country is north of Syria?
- What is the capital of Jordan?
- In which country is the holy city of Mecca?
- How far is it from Mecca to Jerusalem?
- What is the longitude of Aden, Yemen?
- Which sea is close to the Elburz Mountains?
- Which Mediterranean island is in the Middle East?

Regional Facts

Population: 150 million people

Largest Country: Saudi Arabia

Smallest Country: Bahrain

Largest City: Istanbul, Turkey, 5 million people

Highest Mountain: Damavand, Iran, 18, 376 feet (5,601 m)

Longest River: Euphrates, 1,700 miles (2,736 km)

Russia and its neighbors

St. Basil's Cathedral is one of Moscow's most famous landmarks.

Fifteen former communist republics have recently become independent countries. The fifteen republics used to be the Soviet Union (U.S.S.R.). Most of these new countries have formed the Commonwealth of Independent States (CIS). However, the whole area is occupied by over 100 different national groups. More than 60 different languages are spoken; only Russian is spoken everywhere. It is possible that there will continue to be political struggles, and even war, while further new nations try to become independent. The whole area is about 6,214 miles (10,000 km) long and, in some places, over 2,796 miles (4,500 km) wide. Its climate varies from the freezing Arctic wastes of Siberia in the north, where temperatures have been recorded as low as -94°F (-70°C), to the hot, dry areas of the south. Russia has about 80 percent of the population (about 240 million). Its area stretches from the Baltic Sea in the west to the Pacific Ocean in the east. The Ural Mountains divide Russia into a European and Asian country. It is a federal country, which means that it is the union of many national republics.

After Russia, the largest countries are Kazakhstan, Ukraine, Turkmenistan, and Uzbekistan.

Regional Facts

Population: 300 million people

Capital City of Russia: Moscow

Largest City: Moscow, 8 million people

Highest Mountain: Pik Kommunizma, 24, 590 feet (7,495 m)

Longest River: Lena, 2,654 miles (4,271 km) Russia is the largest country in the world.

Activities

- On which sea is Baku?

- Can you find the Black Sea?

- How far is it from Odessa to St. Petersburg?

- In which direction do you travel from Moscow to St. Petersburg?

- Between which two seas are the Caucasus Mountains?

- Which city is farthest west — Kiev, Moscow, or St. Petersburg?

- Which ocean is to the north of Russia?

- Which plateau is above the Arctic Circle?

India and its neighbors

This part of the world is one of great physical contrasts. Northern India, Afghanistan, Pakistan, Bhutan, and Nepal are mountainous. The highest mountain range in the world, the Himalayas, forms a spectacular border between Tibetan China and Nepal and Bhutan.

India, Pakistan, and Bangladesh are densely populated countries. India alone has 750 million people. Most live in villages and work as farmers. Most farms are small, but India grows enough food for all its people.

Most of the rain needed to grow crops falls in just a few weeks of the year. This is called the monsoon. Too much rain means floods; too little, and there will be drought.

Most people belong to one of the many different religions in this region. There are Hindus, Muslims, Parsis, Sikhs, Christians, Buddhists, and many others.

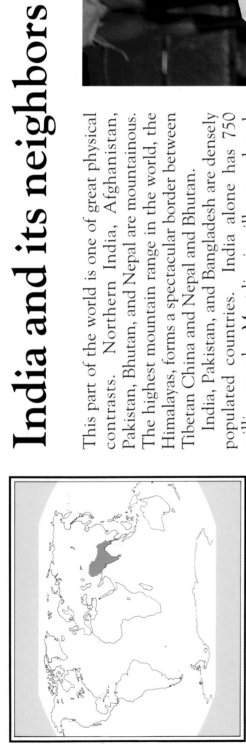

A mother bathes her child in the Ganges River. The Ganges is a sacred river with many holy cities along its banks.

Regional Facts

Population: One billion people

Largest Country: India

Smallest Country: Maldives

Largest City: Calcutta, India, 10 million people

Highest Mountain: Everest, Nepal/Tibet, 29,028 feet (8,848 m) — the highest mountain in the world

Longest River: Indus, 1,800 miles (2,900 km)

Activities

- What is the capital of Sri Lanka?
- Into which bay does the Ganges River flow?
- The second highest mountain in the world is in Pakistan, near the Indian border. What is it called?
- How far is it from Bombay to Calcutta?
- Which country is west of the Thar Desert, India?
- In which sea is the position 25°N, 65°E?
- Which country stretches further south, Bangladesh or Pakistan?
- In which country is Kathmandu?
- To which country do the Andaman Islands belong?

China, Japan, and their neighbors

China is the world's third largest country. It is also the world's most populated country. A main part of the people's diet is rice, which is grown in flooded fields in southern and central China. In the cooler, drier areas of the north and east, farmers grow wheat and corn. China is the world's top producer of cotton and tobacco. While most people work as farmers, many people in today's cities work in factories.

Over its long history, China has often been closed to outsiders. Today, tourists visit the Great Wall, which dates back some 2,200 years and is about 1,500 miles (2,400 km) long.

Japan is the richest country in Asia. It has very successful industries that sell their products all over the world. Since World War II, Japan has become a world leader in producing cars, calculators, pianos, and ships.

Japan is made up of four big islands (Hokkaido, Honshu, Shikoku, and Kyushu) and about 3,000 smaller ones. About fifty of Japan's mountains are active volcanoes. Fujiyama is the highest.

Chinese children are encouraged to exercise at an early age.

Regional Facts

Population: 1.25 billion people

Largest Country: China — the third largest country in the world

Smallest Country: Taiwan

Largest City: Beijing (Peking), China, 9 million people

Highest Mountain: Everest, Tibet/Nepal, 29,028 feet (8,848 m) — the highest mountain in the world

Longest River: Chang Jiang, 3,964 miles (6,380 km) — the third longest river in the world

---

Activities

• Which two countries in the world are larger than China?

• Into which sea does the Chang Jiang river flow?

• In which direction is Taiwan from Hong Kong?

• What is Japan's highest mountain?

• To which country does Hong Kong currently belong?

• How far is it from Shanghai to Hong Kong?

• What is the large desert in southern Mongolia and northern China called?

• What is the Chinese name for the city long called Peking?

• What is the capital of South Korea?

• Which of Japan's four large islands is farthest north?

Right: Tokyo, the capital of Japan, is one of the world's busiest cities.

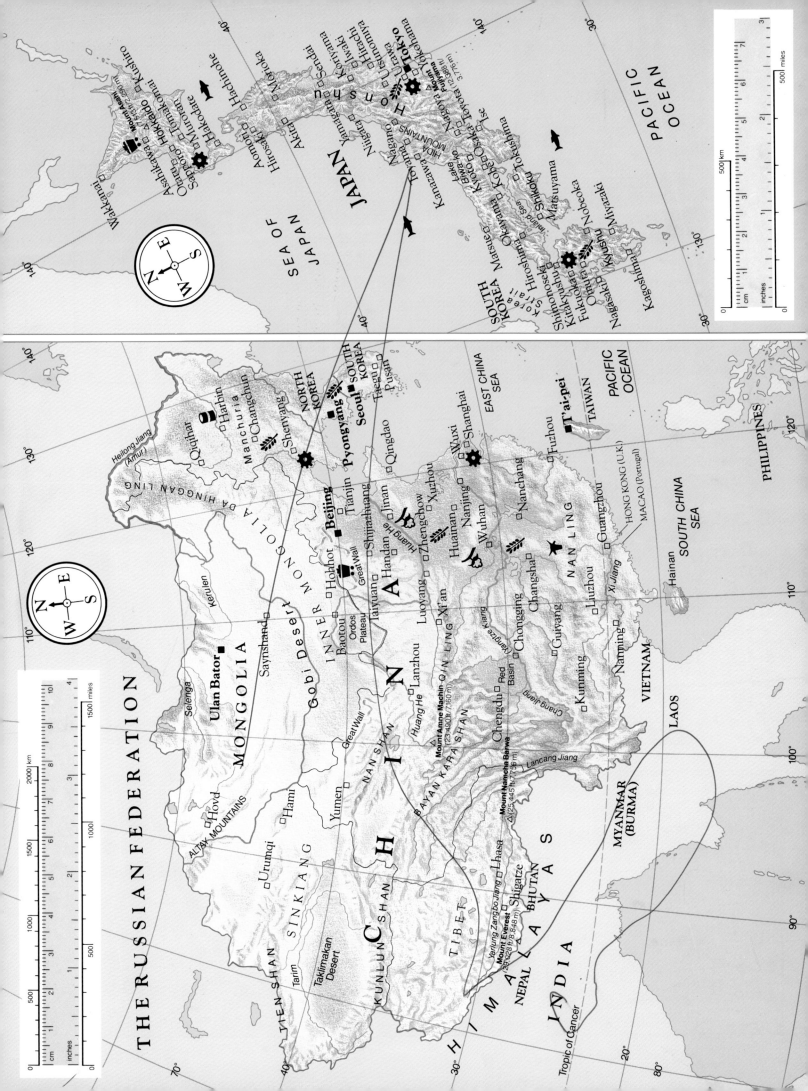

Southeast Asia

These Balinese people are tossing rice to separate the grains.

Much of Southeast Asia is made up of islands. Indonesia has over 13,000 islands, and the Philippines has more than 7,000. Many are volcanic. This region is hot and wet all year round. For a few months each year there is a heavy rain season, called the monsoon.

Many people live in Southeast Asia. The cities are overcrowded with poor people living on the edges of cities in shanty towns. Their homes are made of scrap wood and iron. Most people live on low land near the coast and in river valleys. Many farm the land, growing rice, vegetables, spices, and fruit. Rice is a major food in this region. It is often grown on flat terraces on the sides of hills and mountains. The mountains are covered with thick rain forests. Some of the wood from the trees, such as teak and mahogany, is very valuable. Some trees provide useful materials other than wood.

Sap from the rubber tree, for example, provides rubber. Malaysia, Indonesia, and Thailand are the world's top rubber producers.

Vietnam, Laos, and Cambodia (Kampuchea) are poor countries. They have suffered greatly in recent years from war and political changes.

Music, dance, plays, and handmade crafts keep the ancient legends of Southeast Asia alive. Most of the people are Buddhists or Muslims. Temple dancers tell the stories of their religion as they dance.

Regional Facts

Population: 350 million people

Largest Country: Indonesia

Largest City: Jakarta, Indonesia, 6.5 million people

Smallest Country: Singapore

Longest River: Mekong, 2,600 miles (4,185 km)

Activities

- How far is it across the South China Sea from Da Nang to Manila?
- In which direction do you travel from Ho Chi Minh to Hanoi?
- What is the capital of Thailand?
- Two large and two small Southeast Asian islands are on the Equator. Which are they?
- In which ocean are the Philippines?
- Which strait divides Malaysia from Sumatra?
- Is Bali east, west, north, or south of Java?
- Into which sea does the Mekong River flow?
- Which three countries border on Cambodia (Kampuchea)?
- To which group of islands does Halmahera belong?

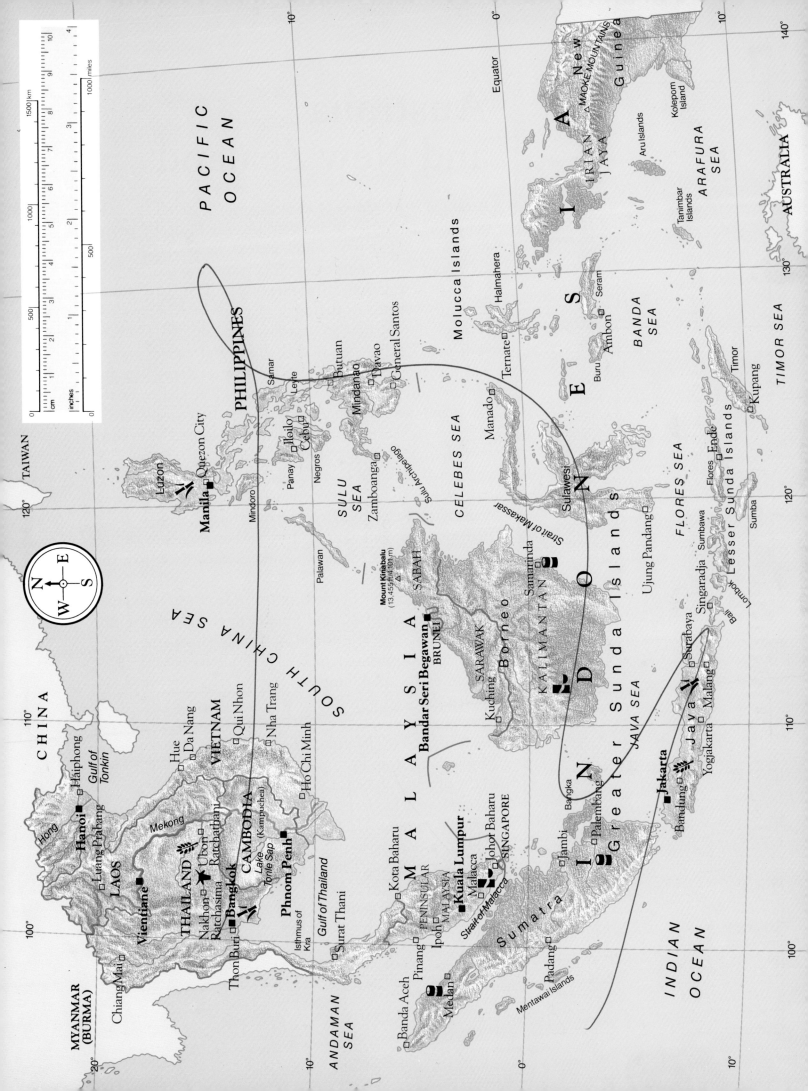

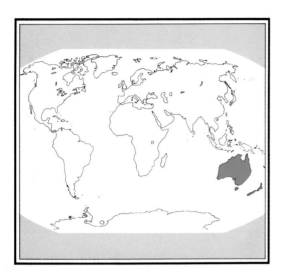

Australia and New Zealand

Australia is a country of contrasts. It is one of the least populated countries in the world, yet most of the people live in crowded towns and cities. It is the smallest continent with the greatest proportion of desert, yet one of the richest nations. It is one of the oldest land masses on Earth, yet one of the last to be developed by people. Perhaps the greatest contrast is between the Outback with its vast, flat desert and sheep and cattle stations and the coastal cities where most Australians live and work. Australia is also the top wool producer in the world and has three times more sheep than people.

The early Australians were the Aborigines. They have been living there for about 30,000 years. About 200 years ago, people from many countries in Europe, especially Britain, settled in what was to them a new country. They brought European lifestyles with them that were very different from the Aboriginal way of life. Major cities, like Melbourne and Sydney, look like the cities of Europe.

The country has a varied climate. Deserts in the center are dry and very hot, and jungles in the north are hot and steamy. On the island of Tasmania, in the south, the temperatures are quite cool with plenty of rain.

The early inhabitants of New Zealand were the Maoris, who came from the Polynesian Islands. People came from Britain in the nineteenth century to start a new life farming and gold mining. Today, New Zealand is a rich farming country. Dairy cattle are raised on North Island, and sheep graze on South Island.

Activities

- In which sea is the Great Barrier Reef?

- Which town is right in the middle of Australia?

- Which is the highest mountain in New Zealand?

- How far is it from Perth to Brisbane?

- In which direction do you travel from Sydney to Melbourne?

- In which Australian state is Brisbane?

Most of the people of Australia live in cities on the coasts.

Regional Facts

Population: Australia, 15 million people
New Zealand, 3.5 million people

Capitals: Australia, Canberra
New Zealand, Wellington

Largest City: Sydney, Australia, 3.5 million people

Highest Mountain: Mt. Cook, New Zealand, 12,346 ft (3,764 m)

Longest River: Darling, Australia, 1,702 miles (2,740 km)

The Pacific Islands

Easter Island is famous for its unusual statues.

Activities

- What is the capital of Tuvalu?
- To which country does Pitcairn Island belong?
- Which continent is to the east of the Galápagos Islands?
- What imaginary line from west to east divides the Pacific Ocean in two?
- Which two countries are separated by the Tasman Sea?
- Which country looks after the Trust Territory of the Pacific Islands?
- What is the capital of Fiji?
- Which is the largest ocean on Earth?

Regional Facts

Population: 5 million people

Largest Country: Papua New Guinea

Smallest Country: Nauru

Moorea, one of the Society Islands.

There are thousands of small islands in the Pacific Ocean. The ocean itself covers almost half the Earth's surface. The Pacific islands fall into three main groups, according to location and the type of people who live on them. The people of Melanesia are very much like the native peoples of Africa. The native Hawaiians and the people of Polynesia are related to Asian peoples. The people of Micronesia represent a mixture of the other two peoples.

Some of the islands are made of coral, the limestone skeletons of tiny sea animals. Many of these islands are very mountainous and were created by volcanoes. The islands that make up Hawaii are volcanic. Hawaii is one of the fifty states of the United States.

Hawaii, Fiji, and Tahiti are popular with tourists, but many of the smaller islands get few visitors. Life on these islands is often very simple. People live in small villages, grow food in gardens, and fish from canoes. On larger islands, people work on banana and cocoa plantations or mine copper and other minerals.

Some groups of islands are still colonies and belong to other countries. Others are independent and have their own governments.

150°

PACIFIC OCEAN

Aleutian Is.

180°

BERING SEA

150°

An aerial view of the Arctic. Notice all the different land masses that surround the northern part of the globe.

120°

ALASKA (U.S.A.)

Yukon

Bering Strait

Wrangel Island

Koyma

S I B E R I A

Barrow

Prudhoe Bay

EAST SIBERIA SEA

Mackenzie

Inuvik

BEAUFORT SEA

New Siberian Islands

Tiksi

Lena

120°

CANADA

Banks Island

LAPTEV SEA

Victoria Island

Queen Elisabeth Islands

ARCTIC OCEAN

Severnaya Zemlya

RUSSIA

Ellesmere Island

LOMONOSOV RIDGE

North Pole

Noril'sk

90°

Yenisei

Thule

Franz Josef Land (U.S.S.R.)

KARA SEA

Baffin Island

BAFFIN BAY

Svalbard (Norway)

Novaya Zemlya

Davis Strait

GREENLAND SEA

BARENTS SEA

90°

GREENLAND (Kalaallit Nunaat)

NORWEGIAN SEA

Murmansk

60°

Arkhangel'sk

ATLANTIC OCEAN

Denmark Strait

Arctic Circle

Narvik

NORWAY

SWEDEN

FINLAND

Ob

30°

ICELAND

| 0 | 500 | 1000 | 1500 | 2000 km |

| cm | 1 | 2 | 3 | 4 | 5 | 6 | 7 |

| inches | | 1 | | 2 | | 3 |

| 0 | | 500 | | 1000 | | 1500 miles |

0°

An aerial view of the Antarctic. Notice how close the tip of South America is to the continent of Antarctica.

ATLANTIC OCEAN

30°

0°

60°

South Georgia
(U.K.)

South Sandwich
Islands
(U.K.)

Falkland Islands
(Islas Malvinas)
(U.K.)

60°

South Orkney
Islands
(U.K.)

Antarctic Circle

Cape Horn

Drake Passage

70°

South Shetland
Islands (U.K.)

Antarctic
Peninsula

WEDDELL SEA

Queen Maud Land

30°

Palmer Land

Coats Land

Alexander
Island

Berkner
Island

80°

Enderby
Land

90°

BELLINGSHAUSEN
SEA

Ronne
Ice Shelf

Ellsworth
Land

△ Vinson Massif
(5140m)

A N T A R C T I C A

MacRobertson
Land

60°

AMUNDSEN
SEA

South Pole

American
Highland

Marie Byrd
Land

TRANSANTARCTIC
Queen Maud Range

90°

120°

Ross Ice Shelf

MOUNTAINS

Wilkes Land

ROSS SEA

Victoria
Land

PACIFIC OCEAN

Terre
Adelie

INDIAN OCEAN

150°

120°

180°

	500	1000	1500	2000	2500 km

cm 1 2 3 4 5 6 7 8 9 10

inches 1 2 3 4

0	500	1000	1500 miles

Map Index